KT-442-977

Funland and Other Poems

Poetry
Walking Under Water
Tenants of the House
Poems, Golders Green
A Small Desperation
Selected Poems

Plays
Three Questor Plays

Novels
Ash on a Young Man's Sleeve
Some Corner of an English Field
O. Jones, O. Jones

General
Medicine on Trial

Dannie Abse

FUNLAND AND OTHER POEMS

 Hutchinson of London

B1

HUTCHINSON & CO (*Publishers*) LTD
3 Fitzroy Square, London W1

London   Melbourne   Sydney   Auckland
Wellington   Johannesburg   Cape Town
and agencies throughout the world

First published 1973

*This book has been set in Bembo, printed in Great Britain
on Antique Wove paper by Benham & Co. Ltd., Colchester,
Essex, and bound by Wm. Brendon & Son Ltd., Tiptree, Essex*

ISBN 0 09 114750 6 (cased)
      0 09 114751 4 (paper)

Joan's

These poems were first published in: *Ambit, Antaeus, The Antioch Review, The American Scholar, Encounter, The Humanist* (U.S.A.), *The New Statesman, Planet, Poetry* (Chicago), *Second Aeon, Shenandoah, The Sunday Times, The Times Literary Supplement, Tribune,* and *Wave.* Acknowledgements are also owed to *Allsorts* (Macmillan), *Corgi Modern Poets in Focus* (No. 4), *Poems 69* (Gwasg Gomer), *Responses* (N.B.L.), *New Poems* (P.E.N.), and also to the B.B.C., which broadcast on Radio 3 an earlier version of the poem *Funland.*

Contents

2 Funland

1 As I was saying

Mysteries

At night, I do not know who I am
when I dream, when I am sleeping.

Awakened, I hold my breath and listen:
a thumbnail scratches the other side of the wall.

At midday, I enter a sunlit room
to observe the lamplight on for no reason.

I should know by now that few octaves can be heard,
that a vision dies from being too long stared at;

that the whole of recorded history even
is but a little gossip in a great silence;

that a magnesium flash cannot illumine,
for one single moment, the invisible.

I do not complain. I start with the visible
and am startled by the visible.

Forgotten

That old country I once said I'd visit
when older. Can no one tell me its name?
Odd, to have forgotten what it is called.
I would recognise the name if I heard it.
So many times I have searched the atlas
with a prowling convex lens—to no avail.

I know the geography of the great world
has changed; the war, the peace, the deletions
of places—red pieces gone forever,
and names of countries altered forever:
Gold Coast Ghana, Persia become Iran,
Siam Thailand, and hell now Vietnam.

People deleted. Must I sleep again to reach it,
to find the back door opening to a field,
a barking of dogs, and a path that leads back?
One night in pain, the dead middle of night,
will I awake again, know who I am,
the man from somewhere else, and the place's name?

An old commitment

Long ago my kinsmen slain in battle,
swart flies on all their pale masks feeding.

I had a cause then. Surely I had a cause?
I was for them and they were for me.

Now, when I recall why, what, who,
I think the thought that is as blank as stone.

Travelling this evening, I focus on the back
of brightness, on that red spot wavering.

Behind it, what have I forgotten? It goes
where the red spot goes, rising, descending.

I only describe a sunset, a car travelling
on a swerving mountain road, that's all.

Arriving too late, I approach the unlit dark.
Those who loiter outside exits and entrances

so sadly, so patiently, even they have departed.
And I am no ghost and this place is in ruins.

'Black,' I call softly to one dead but beloved,
'black, black,' wanting the night to reply . . .

                                        . . . 'Black.'

Demo against the Vietnam war, 1968

Praise just one thing in London, he challenged,
as if everybody, everything, owned a minus,
was damnable, and the Inner Circle led to hell;
and I thought, allowed one slot only,
what, in October, would I choose?

Not the blurred grasslands of a royal, moody park
where great classy trees lurk in mist;
not the secretive Thames either, silvering
its slow knots through the East End—
sooty scenes, good for Antonioni panning soft
atmospheric shots, emblems of isolation,
prologue to the elegiac Square, the house where,
suddenly, lemon oblongs spring to windows.

Nor would I choose the stylised catalogue
of torment in the National Gallery.
Better that tatty group, under Nelson's column,
their home-made banners held aloft,
their small cries of 'Peace, Peace,' impotent;
also the moment with the tannoy turned off,
the thudding wings of pigeons audible,
the shredding fountains, once again, audible.

So praise to the end of the march,
their songs, their jargon, outside the Embassy.
Yes, this I'd choose: their ardour, their naivety,
violence of commitment, cruelty of devotion,
'We shall not be moved, We shall overcome'—
despite sullen police concealed in vans
waiting for arclights to fail, for furtive darkness,
and camera-teams, dismantled, all breezing home.

Haloes

Of course haloes are out of fashion.
The commissar is in the castle,
the haemophylic king plays golf
in exile. Feudal days, no more.
Once martyrs were a glut on the market,
now famine faces sink in Asia;
now lamps switched on in drawing rooms
reveal suffering saints no longer there—
as if they had leapt down from walls
leaving behind them halo-tissue.

Such a round shining on walls!
Such a bleeding of intense light!
And all those haloes in hymns of paint,
in museums, in galleries, counterfeit.
Still we appease the old deities—
else we would be like madmen laughing
in public buildings, apparent joy
where rational people speak in whispers;
else saints would never look so ecstatic
in chiaroscuro, on starvation diet.

The Pope does not eat his own entrails
with a golden fork, nor his secretary
cease from phoning the Stock Exchange.
Haloes set men alight in Prague.
Here crowds prefer to shout, 'Easy, Easy,'
at a poisoned green pitch in floodlight.
Pop star, film star, space man, gangster,
move smilingly from camera to camera
seldom to become ritual torches.
Each worth a million, say the guides.

Rightly we are suspicious of haloes
and heroes, of thorns and royal tiaras.
Day and night, an H-bomb circles the world
and Fatty and his henchmen walk
on marble floors, their heritage.
No wonder important men lift up
their hats politely, revealing bald heads.
No-one minds. Their skins have healed.
Think of wall lamps switched off
savagely, all haloes fleeing.

Moon object

After the astronaut's intrusion of moonlight, after
the metal flag, the computer-speeches—this little booty.

Is it really from the moon? Identify it if you can.
Test it, blue-eyed scientist, between finger and thumb.

Through a rainy city a car continues numb.
Its radio blanks out beneath a bridge.

In a restaurant, your colleague with a cold
is trying to taste his own saliva.

On the school piano, your wife's index finger
sinks the highest note. She hears the sound of felt.

Blue eyes, let your own finger and your thumb
slip and slide about it devilishly.

Don't you feel the gravity of the moon?
Say a prayer for the dead and murmur a vow.

Change your white coat for a purple cloak
and cage yourself a peacock or a gnat.

No, rational, you sniff it. But some holes in your front-brain
have been scooped out. A moon-howling dog would know.

Blue eyes, observe it again. See its dull appearance
and be careful: it could be cursed, it could be sleeping.

[18]

Awake, it might change colour like a lampshade
turned on, seething—suddenly moon-plugged.

Scientist, something rum has happened to you.
Your right and left eyes have been switched around.

Back home, if you dialled your own number now,
a shameless voice would reply, 'Who? Who?'

Peachstone

I do not visit his grave. He is not there.
Out of hearing, out of reach. I miss him here,
seeing hair grease at the back of a chair
near a firegrate where his spit sizzled,
or noting, in the cut-glass bowl, a peach.

For that night his wife brought him a peach,
his favourite fruit, while the sick light glowed,
and his slack, dry mouth sucked, sucked, sucked,
with dying eyes closed—perhaps for her sake—
till bright as blood the peachstone showed.

Three street musicians

Three street musicians in mourning overcoats
worn too long, shake money boxes this morning,
then, afterwards, play their suicide notes.

The violinist in chic, black spectacles, blind,
the stout tenor with a fake Napoleon stance,
and the looney flautist following behind,

they try to importune us, the busy living,
who hear melodic snatches of music hall
above unceasing waterfalls of traffic.

Yet if anything can summon back the dead
it is the old-time sound, old obstinate tunes,
such as they achingly render and suspend:

'The Minstrel Boy', 'Roses of Picardy'.
No wonder cemeteries are full of silences
and stones keep down the dead that they defend.

Stones too light! Airs irresistible!
Even a dog listens, one paw raised, while the stout,
loud man amazes with nostalgic notes—though half boozed

and half clapped out. And, as breadcrumbs thrown
on the ground charm sparrows down from nowhere,
now, suddenly, there are too many ghosts about.

Portrait of the artist as a middle-aged man
(3.30 a.m., January 1st)

Pure Xmas card below—street under snow,
under lamplight. My children curl asleep,
my wife also moans from depths too deep
with all her shutters closed and half her life.
And I? I, sober now, come down the stairs
to eat an apple, to taste the snow in it,
to switch the light on at the maudlin time.

Habitual living room, where the apple-flesh
turns brown after the bite, oh half my life
has gone to pot. And, now, too tired for sleep,
I count up the Xmas cards childishly,
assessing, *Jesus*, how many friends I've got!

A new diary

This clerk-work, this first January chore
of who's in, who's out. A list to think about
when absences seem to shout, Scandal! Outrage!
So turning to the blank, prefatory page
I transfer most of the names and phone tags
from last year's diary. True, Meadway, Speedwell,
Mountview, are computer-changed into numbers,
and already their pretty names begin to fade
like Morwenna, Julie, Don't-Forget-Me-Kate,
grassy summer girls I once swore love to.
These, whispering others and time will date.

Cancelled, too, a couple someone else betrayed,
one man dying, another mind in rags.
And remembering them my clerk-work flags,
bitterly flags, for all lose, no-one wins,
those in, those out, *this* at the heart of things.
So I stop, ask: whom should I commemorate,
and who, perhaps, is crossing out my name now
from some future diary? Oh my God,
Morwenna, Julie, don't forget me, Kate.

Miss Book World

We, the judges, a literary lot,
peep-tom legitimately at these beauties,
give marks for legs and breasts, make remarks
low or pompous like most celebrities;
not that we are, but they imagine us so
who parade blatantly as camera-lights flash
crazily for a glossy page and cash.

Perhaps some girls entered for a giggle,
but all walk slave-like in this ritual fuss
of unfunny compère, funny applause,
spotlit dream-girls displayed, a harem for us;
not that they are, but we imagine them so,
with Miss Book World herself just barely flawed,
almost perfect woman, almost perfect fraud.

The illusion over, half the contestants
still fancy themselves in their knock-out pose,
while we literati return to the real
world of fancy, great poetry and prose;
not that it is, but we imagine it so,
great vacant visions in which we delight,
as if we see the stars not only at night.

The death of aunt Alice

Aunt Alice's funeral was orderly,
each mourner correct, dressed in decent black,
not one balding relative berserk with an axe.
Poor Alice, where's your opera-ending?
For alive you relished high catastrophe,
your bible Page One of a newspaper.

You talked of typhoid when we sat to eat;
Fords on the M4, mangled, upside down,
just when we were going for a spin;
and, at London airport, as you waved us off,
how you fatigued us with 'metal fatigue',
vague shapes of Boeings bubbling under seas.

Such disguises and such transformations!
Even trees were but factories for coffins,
rose bushes decoys to rip boys' eyes with thorns.
Sparrows became vampires, spiders had designs,
and your friends also grew SPECTACULAR,
none to bore you by dying naturally.

A. had both kidneys removed in error
at Guy's. 'And such a clever surgeon too.'
B., one night, fell screaming down a liftshaft.
'Poor fellow, he never had a head for heights.'
C., so witty, so feminine, 'Pity
she ended up in a concrete-mixer.'

But now, never again, Alice, will you utter
gory admonitions as some do oaths.
Disasters that lit your eyes will no more
unless, trembling up there, pale saints listen
to details of their bloody martyrdoms,
all their tall stories, your eternity.

Car journeys

Me! dutiful son going back to South Wales, this time afraid
to hear my mother's news. Too often, now, her friends
    are disrobed,
and my aunts and uncles, too, go into the hole, one by one.
The beautiful face of my mother is in its ninth decade.

Each visit she tells me the monotonous story of clocks.
'Oh dear,' I say, or 'how funny,' till I feel my hair turning
    grey
for I've heard that perishable one two hundred times before—
like the rugby 'amateurs' with golden sovereigns in their
    socks.

Then the Tawe ran fluent and trout-coloured over stones
    stonier,
more genuine; then Annabella, my mother's mother,
    spoke Welsh
with such an accent the village said, 'Tell the truth, fach,
you're no Jewess. *They're* from the Bible. *You're* from
    Patagonia!'

I'm driving down the M4 again under bridges that leap
over me then shrink in my side mirror. Ystalyfera is farther
than smoke and God further than all distance known. I
    whistle
no hymn but an old Yiddish tune my mother knows.
    It won't keep.

[27]

2 *Incident on a summer night*

The route not even in the A.A. book.
I'm nowhere, I thought, driving slowly
because of the raw surface of the lane
that developed between converging hedges;
then, soon, fabulous in the ghastly wash
of headlights, a naked man approached
crying without inhibition, one hand to his face,
his somehow familiar mouth agape.

Surely he could see me?
From the two moth-filled headlights
surely he would draw back, change his pace?
This road to Paradise, I muttered.
At last I passed him or say, rather, he passed me.
Afterwards, the accelerating lane widened
and long lights fumbled, momentarily,
hedges, hurtling gate, country wall, amazing tree.

3 *I sit in my parked car*

And they, too, seem like images from sleep:
this Asian child and shadow
playing on a rubbish heap;
that old man incognito
preaching to the pigeons.
'Kill the Reds,' he says, 'kill the Reds.'
I wind up the car window.

Nearby, sunlight on a broken bottle
throws trinket colours on a stone,
but the ancient man in smoked glasses
walks to the right alone
mouthing a forgotten language,
walks out of sight, off the page.

And I? I leave the car, feel dizzy—
even the plastic seating's hot.
Grounded pigeons purr their gutturals,
the pistons in their heads are busy.
When the door slams its small shot
the pigeons reach for the sky,
the shadow chases the child.

In Hotel Insomnia, once, at dawn,
I thought I heard those pigeons' wings
whirring outside my numbered door.
It was only the lift gone wild.
Up and down on a nightmare ride
its gates opened at each floor,
gates of ivory or of horn:
no Asian child, nor ancient man,
nobody at all inside.

4 Driving home

Opposing carbeams wash my face.
Such flickerings hypnotise. To keep awake
I listen to the B.B.C. through cracklings
of static, fade-outs under bridges,
to a cool expert who, in lower case,
computes and graphs 'the ecological
disasters that confront the human race.'

Almost immediately (ironically?),
I see blue flashing lights ahead and brake
before a car accordioned, floodlit, men heaving
at a stretcher, an ambulance oddly angled, tame, in wait.
Afterwards, silent, I drive home cautiously
where, late, the eyes of my youngest child
flicker dreamily, and are full of television.

'He's waited up,' his mother says, 'to say goodnight.'
My son smiles briefly. Such emotion! I surprise
myself and him when I hug him tight.

A note left on the mantelpiece
(*For his wife*)

Attracted by their winning names I chose
Little Yid and *Welsh Bard*; years later backed
the swanky jockeys, and still thought I lacked
inspiration, the uncommon touch, not
mere expertise. Each way, I paid in prose.

Always the colours and stadiums beckoned
till, on the nose, at Goodwood, the high gods
jinxed the favourite despite the odds.
Addict that I was, live fool and dead cert.
His velvet nostrils lagged a useless second.

A poet should have studied style not form
(sweet, I regret the scarcity of roses)
but by Moses and by the nine Muses
I'll no more. Each cruising nag is a beast
so other shirts can keep the centaur warm.

Adieu, you fading furlongs of boozing,
hoarse voices at Brighton, white rails, green course.
Conclusion? Why, not only the damned horse
but whom it's running against matters.
By the way, apologies for losing.

A faithful wife

(A letter written by an Egyptian lady during the reign of Amenhotep III, about 1385 B.C.E.)

To my husband, my lord,
whose caravans lodge in Canaan,
whose sperm has not stiffened,
for three long months, my bed-linen,
say:
at the feet of my husband,
as before the king, the sun-god,
seven times and seven times
I fall.
For I am an obedient
of my husband, my lord.

When I keep my head still
moving my two eyes this way
it is dark;
when I keep my head still
moving my two eyes that way
it is dark;
but when I gaze in front,
towards my lord, it is dazzle,
it is the spirit on the wall
flat as a sunbeam:
it is the time of the short shadows.

Further: all seems tasteless
like the white of an egg
since my lord departed.
Thus ask my falcon, my husband,
to send for his servant, as promised,
to journey on the stony heat
across the camel-coloured desert
even to the shrewd wells.
For I have placed the yoke
of my husband, my lord,
upon my neck and I bear it.

In the whirling dust-storm,
a brick may move
from beneath its companions.
When the night grows with jackals
a dog may move
from his sick master.
But send for me and I shall not move
from beneath the shadow
of my husband, my lord,
as that shadow will not move
from his two feet.

Yet my lord sends no report,
neither good nor evil.
Has he gone to the land of Hatti,
or to the region of the bedouins?
Does he take care of his chariot?
When the first three stars appear
does he sleep each evening
with a piece of wool upon him?
Or has the foe raided his caravans,
the night guards drunk, my lord inert?
Very anxious is thy servant.

Oh may this tablet find him safe
in Joppa, in the meadows
blossoming in their season:
else let the dust follow his chariot
like smoke, and let the god, Amon, keep
all those tracks that zag between
the rising and the setting sun
free from ambuscade,
free for my lord whose speeches are
gathered together on my tongue,
and remain upon my lips.

100 hats

(Adapted from the Hebrew of Amir Gilboa)

To balance one hundred hats on my head
100 hats   100 colours
a hundred hats a hundred colours and shades of colour
one hundred hats incandescent with colour

if there were one hundred hats on my head
how I would move with the crowd to the Square
and the people spread open like a fan for me
that I should throw up my hats in the air

if there were one hundred hats on my head
a hundred hats a hundred colours and shades of colour
with the high sun glossing my hundred hats
with the high sun sparkling my hundred colours

how admiringly the people would say to me
100 people   in   100 hats
'hooray' and 'goal' and 'well done' and 'hooray'
and jump with joy with each of my gay flying hats.

Here

In the precincts of cautious Golders Green,
at a front gate, my companion and I
hardly noticed the tidy, mowed gardens
of 3 p.m., the hydrangeas, the sign
FOR SALE, a parked car in steady sunlight.
Simply, we were about to say, 'goodbye,'
when suddenly, startled, we saw unlikely
down the empty street, flouncing towards us
the ribboned horse and cart, the fat driver

solemn, outrageous, in a tall top hat,
garbed in funeral satin black—and in the cart
a brightness of balloons, a batty cargo,
slowly slowly bouncing, light as moon-air,
all the colours of a festival.
The driver did not smile, did not raise his hat,
jogging down the afternoon, going where,
deaf to our world, the afternoon must go.

Since then, 1000 afternoons have gone
unremarkably, and still I savour
its bland mystery, the oddness of it,
the unfathomable, blind, rare uses
I may make of it: that something not dreamt,
I swear I swear, something not fantasy,
not film shot—though, now, true fancy ablaze,
I see one fat reader lift his ancient eyes,
deaf to our world, and raise his tall black hat.

[37]

The bereaved

Once his voice had been so thrilling,
the twelve women all agreed. Off and on TV
he was charming, he was charismatic,
yet without side. He was their pin-up.

But now his incomprehensible language
when he spoke (which was rare);
the way he would stare into chasms of space
as if Eurydice were there; or would suddenly

howl out an emptiness—that was too much
(a man should not dream of maggots too long)
that was ridiculous, even frightening, they said,
the twelve women, reasonably moving towards him.

2

Twelve women pulling him,
twelve women screaming,
kicking, scratching, pulling at him,
until on the ground, at last,
he was being smothered,
bitten by women's teeth,
his eyes pushed in by women's thumbs.

Afterwards, the cyanosed figure
on the ground, what was left of him,
striped with blood, did not move,
and the women stood back silent,
most of them already smoking
and the others lighting up.

Explanation of a news item

Police Constable Appleton said, 'At eight o'clock in the morning the children looked through the railings and saw him walking slowly through the cemetery.'

He leading, they floated up
in slow motion, as if under water
(though there was no water)
to the small, bright oblong above,
'Are you ready?' he asked,
with outstretched hand blindly.
'I must not,' he heard her whisper,
'I am but a ghost, a glitter on dust
fading in the upper light.'
He did not understand: he turned,
he looked down into the dark,
he looked aghast—and suddenly
her voice plunging cried out
like an echo of an echo of an echo,
so that he awoke startled
in the February sunlight,
walking on the gravel pathway
between the stone-eyed angels
and the nicely ordered graves.

No more Mozart

High to the right a hill of trees,
a fuselage of branches,
reflects German moonlight
like dull armour.
Sieg heil!

Higher still, one moon migrates deathwards,
a white temper between clouds.
To the left, the other slides
undulating on the black
oiled, rippling reservoir.

Can't sleep for Mozart,
and on the winter glass
a shilling's worth of glitter.

The German streets tonight
are soaped in moonlight.
The streets of Germany are clean
like the hands of Lady Macbeth.

Back in bed the eyes close, do not sleep.
Achtung! Achtung!
Someone is breathing nearby,
someone not accounted for,
like a ghost on barbed wire,
someone dumb, it seems.
The gasmask goggles on a skull.

Now, of course, no more Mozart.
With eyes closed still
the body touches itself, takes stock.
Above the hands the thin wrists
attached to them; and on the wrists
the lampshade material.
Also the little hairs that can be pulled.

The eyes open:
the German earth is made of helmets;
the wind seeps through a deep
frost hole that is somewhere else
carrying the far Jew-sounds of railway trucks.

Nothing is annulled:
the blood vow, the undecorated cry,
someone robbed of his name,
a grenade, a decapitation,
and the wind-pipe whistling.
Then silence again.

Afterwards:
the needle rests on a record
with nothing on that record turning,
neither sound nor silence,
nothing at all,
for it is sleep at last.

There, the fugitive body has arrived
at the stink of nothing.
And twelve million eyes
in six million heads
stare in the same direction.

Outside, the electrician works
inside his cloud, silently,
and the reservoir darkens.

Germany 1970

The case

From the ward's far window he stared
through the weighted trees at the tennis court,
its ground red as Devonshire, old rusted blood.
His own had been syringed, drawn off many times,
I learnt from the tall doctor, my colleague,
for sedimentation rates, white cell counts,
haemoglobin content, clotting time,
bleeding time, agglutination tests,
many blood-cultures over many months.
For the patient had been ill many months,
sometimes feeling better, out of bed,
watching the sunlight altering the lawns
or rain in the tennis court. Now, on the grass,
leaves had settled, orange brown yellow,
soaked chemically, dyed in autumn blood.
'Let me speak to your patient then,' I said,
and on the walls the sunlight fused abruptly.
'What's his name?' My colleague had not understood
who knew the man's heart but not the man.
Smiling at rows of beds we walked on
parquet floors, up the ward, and I shook hands
with a shadow. 'Good morning, John,' I said,
reading his name on the temperature chart.

Miracles

Last night, the priest dreamed he quit his church
at midnight, and then saw vividly
a rainbow in the black sky.
I said, every day, you can see
conjunctions equally odd—awake and sane, that is—
a tangerine on the snow, say.
Such things are no more incredible than God.

Such things, said the priest, do not destroy a man,
but seeing a rainbow in the night sky
—awake and sane, that is—why, doctor,
like a gunshot that could destroy a man.
That would not allow him to believe in anything,
neither to praise nor blame. A doctor must believe
in miracles but I, a priest, dare not.

Then my incurable cancer patient,
the priest, sat up in bed, looked to the window,
and peeled his tangerine, silently.

In the theatre

(A true incident)

'Only a local anaesthetic was given because of the blood
pressure problem. The patient, thus, was fully awake
throughout the operation. But in those days—in 1938,
in Cardiff, when I was Lambert Rogers' dresser—they
could not locate a brain tumour with precision. Too much
normal brain tissue was destroyed as the surgeon crudely
searched for it, before he felt the resistance of it . . . all
somewhat hit and miss. One operation I shall never
forget. . . .'
                                        (Dr. Wilfred Abse)

Sister saying—'Soon you'll be back in the ward,'
sister thinking—'Only two more on the list,'
the patient saying—'Thank you, I feel fine';
small voices, small lies, nothing untoward,
though, soon, he would blink again and again
because of the fingers of Lambert Rogers,
rash as a blind man's, inside his soft brain.

If items of horror can make a man laugh
then laugh at this: one hour later, the growth
still undiscovered, ticking its own wild time;
more brain mashed because of the probe's braille path;
Lambert Rogers desperate, fingering still;
his dresser thinking, 'Christ! Two more on the list,
a cisternal puncture and a neural cyst.'

[46]

Then, suddenly, the cracked record in the brain,
a ventriloquist voice that cried, 'You sod,
leave my soul alone, leave my soul alone,'—
the patient's dummy lips moving to that refrain,
the patient's eyes too wide. And, shocked,
Lambert Rogers drawing out the probe
with nurses, students, sister, petrified.

'Leave my soul alone, leave my soul alone,'
that voice so arctic and that cry so odd
had nowhere else to go—till the antique
gramophone wound down and the words began
to blur and slow, '. . . leave . . . my . . . soul . . . alone . . .'
to cease at last when something other died.
And silence matched the silence under snow.

Trailer

Nobody's about. It is 1970+.
The occupant has gone. Perhaps temporarily.
The furniture is benumbed, even paralysed.
The flowers in the vase have not quite withered.

Probably the telephone will harangue the objects
in an hour or two, expecting to be answered.
Gradually, it will become less confident, more self-
conscious, aware of its own brittle, fussy clamour.

The provincial anger of the telephone will fatigue
and a man, somewhere else, will blink in a hallway,
will walk on parquet floors, his raised right hand
warmer than the plastic handle of a door.

Meanwhile, the phone here, in this room,
will resume the silence of afterwards.

2 Funland

1 The superintendent

With considerable poise
the superintendent
has been sitting for hours now
at the polished table.

Outside the tall window
all manner of items
have been thundering down
boom boom stagily
the junk of heaven.

A harp with the nerves missing
the somewhat rusty
sheet iron wings of an angel
a small bent tubular hoop
still flickering flickering
like fluorescent lighting
when first switched on
that old tin lizzie banger
Elijah's burnt-out chariot
various other religious hardware
and to cap it all
you may not believe this
a red Edwardian pillar box.

My atheist uncle has been standing
in the corner wrathfully.
Fat Blondie in her pink
transparent nightdress
has been kneeling
on the brown linoleum.

And for some queer reason
our American guest yells
from time to time Mari-*an*
if they give you chewing gum
. . . . CHEW.

Meanwhile the superintendent
a cautious man usually
inclined for instance
to smile in millimetres
has begun to take a great risk.

Calm as usual
masterful as usual
he is drawing the plans of the void
working out it classical proportions.

2 Anybody here seen any Thracians?

The tall handsome man
whom the superintendent
has nicknamed Pythagoras
asked fat Blondie
as she reclined strategically
under the cherry blossom
to join his Society.

The day after that
despite initial fleerings
my uncle also agreed.
The day following another hundred.
Two more weeks everyone
had signed on the dotted line.

There are very few rules.
Members promise to abstain
from swallowing beans. They promise
not to pick up what has fallen
never to stir a fire with an iron
never to eat the heart of animals
never to walk on motorways
never to look in a mirror
that hangs beside a light.
All of us are happy with the rules.

But Pythagoras is not happy.
He wanted to found
a Society not a Religion
and a Society he says
washing his hands with moonlight
in a silver bowl
has to be exclusive.
Therefore someone must be banned.
Who? Who? Tell us Pythagoras.
The Thracians yes the Thracians.

But there are no Thracians among us.
We look left and right wondering
who of us could be a secret Thracian
wondering
who of us would say
with the voice of insurrection
I love you
not in a bullet proof room
and not with his eyes closed.

Pythagoras also maintains
that Thracians have blue hair and red eyes.
Now all day we loiter near the gates
hoping to encounter someone of this description
so that what is now a Religion
can triumphantly become a Society.

3 The summer conference

On grassy lawns
modern black-garbed priests
and scientists in long white coats
confer and dally.

Soon the superintendent will begin
his arcane disquisition
on the new bizarre secret weapon.
(Pssst—the earwigs of R.A.F. Odiham)
Meanwhile I—surprise surprise—
observe something rather remarkable
over there.

Nobody else sees it (near the thornbush)
the coffin rising out of the ground
the old smelly magician himself no less
rising out of the coffin.

He gathers about him his mothy purple cloak.

Daft and drunk with spells
he smiles lopsidedly.
His feet munch on gravel.

He is coming he is coming here
(Hi brighteyes! Hiya brighteyes!)
he is waving that unconvincing
wand he bought in Woolworths.
He has dipped it in a luminous
low-grade oil pool.
Bored with his own act he shouts
JEHOVAH ONE BAAL NIL

Then a lightning flash ha ha
a bit of a rumble of thunder.
Nothing much you understand.
Why should the aged peacock
stretch his wings?

At once the scientists take off
the priests hurry up
into the sky. They zoom.
They free-wheel high over rooftops
playing guitars;
they perform exquisite
figures of 8
but the old mediocre reprobate
merely shrinks them
then returns to his smelly coffin.
Slowly winking he pulls down the lid
slowly the coffin sinks into the ground.
(Bye brighteyes! Arrivederci brighteyes!)

I wave. I blink.
The thunder has cleared
the summer afternoon is vacated.
As if a cannon had been fired
doves and crows
circle the abandoned green lawns.

4 The poetry reading

Coughing and echo of echoes.
A lofty resonant public place.
It is the assembly hall.
Wooden chairs on wooden planks.
Suddenly he enters suddenly
a hush but for the small
distraction of one chair
squeaking in torment on a plank
then his voice unnatural.

He is an underground vatic poet.
His purple plastic coat is enchanting.
Indeed he is chanting
'Fu-er-uck Fu-er-uck'
with spiritual concentration.
Most of us laugh
because the others are laughing
most of us clap
because the others are clapping.

In the Interval out of focus
in the foyer Mr Poet signs his books.
My atheist uncle asseverates
that opus you read Fuck Fuck—
a most affecting and effective
social protest Mr Poet.

In the ladies' corner though
Marian eyeing the bard
maintains he is a real
sexual messiah
that his poem was not an expletive
but an incitement.
Fat Blondie cannot cease from crying.
She thinks his poem so nostalgic.

Meanwhile the superintendent asks
Mr Poet what is a poem?
The first words Eve spoke to Adam?
The last words Adam spoke to Eve
as they slouched from Paradise?

Mr Poet trembles
he whistles
he shakes his head Oi Oi.
As if his legs were under water
he lifts up and down in slow motion
up and down his heavy feet
he rubs the blood vessels in his eyes
he punches with a steady rhythm
his forehead
and then at last
there is the sound of gritty clockwork
the sound of a great whirring.

He is trying to say something.

[58]

His sputum is ostentatious
his voice comes through the long ago.

After the interval
the hall clatters raggedly into silence.
Somewhere else distant
a great black bell is beating
the sound of despair
and then is still.
Cu-er-unt Cu-er-unt chants the poet.
We applaud politely
wonder whether he is telling or asking.
The poet retires a trifle ill.
We can all see that he requires air.

5 Visiting day

The superintendent told us
that last summer on vacation
he saw a blind poet
reading Homer
on a Greek mountainside.

As a result my atheist uncle
has fitted black lenses
into his spectacles.
They are so opaque
he cannot see through them.
He walks around with a white stick.
We shout Copycat Copycat.

In reply his mouth utters
I don't want to see I can't bear to see
any more junk dropping down.
Meanwhile visitors of different sizes
in circumspect clothes in small groups
are departing from the great lawns—
though one alone lags behind and is waving.

She in that blue orgone dress waving
reminds me how I wrote a letter once.
'Love read this though it has little meaning
for by reading this you give me meaning'
I wrote or think I wrote or meant to write
and receiving no reply I heard
the silence.
Now I see a stranger waving.

October evenings are so moody.
A light has gone on
in the superintendent's office.
There are rumours that next week
all of us will be issued
with black specs.

Maybe yes maybe no.

But now the gates have closed
now under the huge unleafy trees
there is nobody.
Father father there is no-one.
We are only middle-aged.
There are too many ghosts already.
We remain behind like evergreens.

6 Autumn in Funland

These blue autumn days
we turn on the water taps.
Morse knockings in the pipes
dark pythagorean
interpretations.

The more we know
the more we journey into ignorance.

All day mysterious aeroplanes
fly over
leaving theurgic vapour trails
dishevelled by the wind
horizontal chalky lines
from some secret script
announcing names perhaps
of those about to die.

Downstairs the superintendent
sullen as a ruined millionaire
says nothing does nothing
stares through the dust-flecked window.
He will not dress a wound even.
He cannot stop a child from crying.

Again at night
shafting through the dark
on the bedroom walls
a veneer wash of radium
remarkably disguised
as simple moonlight.
My vertebral column
is turning into glass.

O remember
the atrocities of the Thracians.
They are deadly cunning.
Our water is polluted.
Our air is polluted.
Soon our orifices will bleed.

These black revolving nights
we are all funambulists.
The stars below us
the cerebellum disordered
we juggle on the edge of the earth
one foot on earth
one foot over the abyss.

7 Death of the superintendent

With considerable poise
in a darkening room
the superintendent sat immobile
for hours at the polished table.
His heart had stopped in the silence
between two beats.

Down with the Thracians.
Down with the Thracians
who think God has blue hair and red eyes.
Down with the bastard Thracians
who somehow killed our superintendent.

Yesterday the morning of the funeral
as instructed by Pythagoras
all members on waking kept their eyes closed
all stared at the blackness
in the back of their eyelids
all heard far away five ancient sounds fading.

Today it's very cold.
Fat Blondie stands inconsolable
in the middle of the goldfish pool.
She will not budge.
The musky waters have amputated her feet.
Both her eyes are crying simultaneously.
She hold her shoes in her right hand
and cries and cries.

Meantime our American guest tries
the sophistry of a song.
The only happiness we know she sings
is the happiness that's gone
and Mr Poet moans like a cello
that's most itself when most melancholy.

To all of this
my atheist uncle responds magnificently.
In his funeral black specs
he will be our new leader.
Look how spitting on his hands first
he climbs the flagpole.
Wild at the very top he shouts
I AM IMMORTAL.

8 Lots of snow

First the skies losing height
then snow raging and the revolution bungled.
Afterwards in the silence
between two snowfalls
we deferred to our leader.
We are but shrubs not tall cedars.

Let Pythagoras be
an example to all Thracian spies
my tyrant uncle cried
retiring to the blackness inside
a fat Edwardian pillar box.

Who's next for the icepick?

Already the severed head of Pythagoras
transforms the flagpole
into a singularly
long white neck.

It has become a god that cannot see
how the sun drips its dilutions
on dumpy snowacres.

And I? I write a letter to someone nameless
in white ink on white paper
to an address unknown.
Oh love I write
surely love was no less
because less uttered or more accepted?

My bowels are made of glass.
The western skies try to rouge the snow.
I goosestep across this junk of heaven
to post my blank envelope.

Slowly night begins in the corner
where two walls meet.
The cold is on the crocus.
Snows mush and melt
and small lights fall from twigs.

Bright argus-eyed the thornbush.

Approaching the pillar box
I hear its slit of darkness screaming.

9 The end of Funland

Uncle stood behind me
when I read Mr Poet's poster
on the billiard cloth
of the noticeboard:
COME TO THE THORNBUSH TONIGHT
HEAR THE VOICES ENTANGLED IN IT
MERLIN'S
MESMER'S
ALL THE UNSTABLE MAGICIANS
YEH YEH
DR BOMBASTUS TOO
FULL SUPPORTING CAST.

Not me I said thank you no
I'm a rational man touch wood.
Mesmer is dead these many years
and his purple cloak in rags.

They are all dead replied uncle
don't you know yet
            all of them dead—
gone where they don't play billiards
haven't you heard the news?

And Elijah the meths drinker
what about Elijah I asked
who used to lie on a parkbench
in bearded sleep—he too?

Of course sneered uncle
smashed smashed years ago like the rest of them
gone with the ravens gone with the lightning.
Why else each springtime
with the opening of a door
no-one's there?

Now at the midnight ritual
we invoke Elijah Merlin Mesmer the best of them
gone with the ravens gone with the lightning
as we stand as usual in concentric circles
around the thornbush.
Something will happen tonight.

Next to me fat Blondie sobs.
Latterly she is much given to sobbing.
The more she sobs the more she suffers.

Suddenly above us
frightful insane
the full moon breaks free from a cloud
stares both ways
and the stars in their stalls tremble.

It enters the black arena aghast
at being seen and by what it can see.
It hoses cold fire over the crowd
over the snowacres of descending
unending slopes.

At last in the distance we hear
the transmigration of souls
like clarinets untranquil played by ghosts
that some fools think to be the wind.

Fat Blondie stops her crying
tilts her face towards me amazed
and holds my hand as if I too were dying.
For a moment I feel as clean as snow.

Do not be misled I say
sometimes Funland can be beautiful.
But she takes her hand away.

I can see right through her.
She has become luminous glass.
She is dreaming of the abyss.
We are all dreaming of the abyss
when we forget what we are dreaming of.

But now this so-called moonlight
is changing us all to glass.
We must disperse say goodbye.
We cannot see each other.
Goodbye Blondie goodbye uncle goodbye.

Footsteps in the snow
resume slowly up the slope.

They gave me chewing gum so I chewed.

Who's next for the icepick?

Tell me are we ice or are we glass?

Ask Abaris who stroked my gold thigh.

Fu-er-uck fu-er-uck.

Do not wake us. We may die.